6 KEY NUMBERS EVERY ENTREPRENEUR SHOULD KNOW

How to bring financial clarity to your business

First Edition

By Brooke Lively

6 KEY NUMBERS EVERY ENTREPRENEUR SHOULD KNOW

How to bring financial clarity to your business

First Edition

By

Brooke Lively

CATHEDRAL CAPITAL

201 Main Street
Suite 1260
Fort Worth, Texas 76102
817.338.1101
817.338.1050 (FAX)
Info@CathCap.com

Copyright © 2013-2014 Cathedral Capital, Inc.
Fort Worth, Texas
All Rights Reserved

2026718

DEC 0 3 2014

Table of Contents

Introduction	1
#1. Cash Position	5
#2. Budget	7
#3. Accounts Receivable	11
#4. Cash Projections	16
#5. Budget Variance Report	24
#6. Income Variance Report	27
#7. Balance Sheet	30
Conclusion	32
About the Author	35
Disclaimer	36

To bring financial clarity to your business,
call Cathedral Capital, Inc. at 817.338.1011

Introduction

Think back to the day that you decided to pursue the entrepreneurial path. What dreams and visions motivated you? Why did you renounce the safe, presumably easier path of being someone else's employee to take on the risk of owning and running a business?

Maybe you hoped to achieve financial independence and have more time off. Perhaps you had a crazy, but not totally unfounded, belief that your work could change the world and add substantial value to people's lives.

Unfortunately, as you already know, the entrepreneurial path is paved with obstacles. It takes more than just talent, ambition, resourcefulness, and luck to get things off the ground and keep them in the air. Dun & Bradstreet, a renowned research firm, found that 90% of small businesses fail, and when they do, it's because of a lack of skill and knowledge on the part of the business owner. That is a sobering statistic.

So what skills and knowledge are missing from *your* entrepreneurial toolset? How can you acquire those competences and leverage them to win in business?

There is good news, at least from a financial perspective: there are just **six key numbers** that you need to know, track, and use in your business. Follow these, and you will...

- Vastly increase your likelihood of success;
- Eliminate doubt and uncertainty from your planning;
- Hire and fire better;
- Market more effectively;
- Position your business to be saleable; and
- Enjoy the road ahead!

Think about it this way. Imagine that you own an amazing A/V system with astonishing sound technology, a movie-theater sized flat screen TV and a state-of-the-art digital projector, but you still connect to the web with the same dial-up modem you bought way back when you used AOL. Theoretically, you could still watch and listen to entertainment. But it would take hours to load even the first minute of a movie trailer, and no one would ever want to watch anything at your place.

Metaphorically speaking, knowing and using the six key numbers is like switching from a dial-up modem to a lightning-fast web connection.

When you manage your business by these numbers, your day-to-day experience will be clearer and more harmonious. You'll waste less time and experience less frustration. The whole entrepreneurial journey will be a lot more fun, exciting, and energetic.

Origin of the Six Key Numbers

The six metrics covered were not plucked randomly. Our firm has the privilege of working with tremendously enthusiastic, creative, and gifted entrepreneurs in diverse sectors, helping them manage via this philosophy.

Whether you're in the initial phases of growth—you're still trying to get a handle on cash flow and stay alive from quarter-to-quarter—or you've already built a profitable business that you want to take to the next level, get ready! This brief primer can eliminate your feelings of frustration and give you back peace of mind and control.

So what are these six numbers? Why do you need to track and manage them? What can they do for your business? We'll cover each one in depth, but here's a quick overview:

1. Cash Position

If your business runs out of cash at the wrong time, the consequences can be dire.

How do you track how much cash you really have? Can't your bank statement just tell you?

Actually, no! The amount of money in your business bank account does *not* accurately reflect your cash position. For instance, let's say you wrote a large check to a subcontractor two months ago, but it has not been cashed yet. Now imagine if that check clears right before you must make payroll for two-dozen employees. An incomplete understanding of your cash position can leave you fatally exposed to these types of scenarios.

We'll cover how to identify and track your cash balance the right way, so you stay safe.

2. Budget

You need to know what's in the bank. You also need to know how that money will fund your business activities. A budget assesses where your cash goes and why, much like a dashboard panel on an airplane assesses where the plane goes and why. Would you fly on a plane, if the pilot never looked at the dashboard panel? Hopefully not. Likewise, you shouldn't invest in (much less own) a business that lacks an itemized, clarified budget.

Some of the key numbers to track include:

- Payroll;
- Rent;
- Office supplies;
- Utilities;
- Equipment rentals; and/or
- Insurance.

You also need to include your salary in the monthly nut, unless you want to work for free—not generally advised, unless you have a hefty trust fund or rich uncle willing to support you in perpetuity.

3. Accounts Receivable (A/R) Report

Right now, how much money do your clients owe you? Perhaps you stand to collect tens of thousands of dollars over the next few months. You may be feeling pretty good, because you "know" that cash will come in shortly.

If you have this mindset about A/R, don't be ashamed—many entrepreneurs do. But when you use A/R as a rainy day fund or savings account, effectively what you're doing is providing an unsecured, zero interest loan to your clients.

Also, this approach leads to hidden opportunity costs that can stunt your business.

We'll set the record straight about A/R and help you establish effective processes to protect your personal financials and liberate cash tied up in A/R to build up your business.

4. Cash Projections/Cash Flow Forecast

How much cash will you have on hand next week? How about next month? How about six months from now? Your accounts receivable flows into your cash projections, which in turn help you determine the tipping point for profitability.

Often, business owners think they have "strategy problems," when what they really have is a lack of clarity about their core financials. This fogginess inhibits them from making decisions about how to compete. For instance, let's say you have a great idea for a new product, but it's going to take six months to develop it. During that incubation period, you need to turn down production to a low boil, so your team can focus on research and development (R&D). Do you have enough of a safety net to take this risk?

President Eisenhower once observed that "plans change, but planning is essential." The purpose of planning is to prepare for unseen contingencies so you can improvise better. To that end, you need to update your forecasts on the fly to keep pace with events. If you have accurate cash projections, you won't have to guess – *you will know* – and this knowledge will empower you to take risks to grow the company. In addition, your confidence—which flows from your cash projections—will reduce stress on your employees and spark a more relaxed, creative environment. It's a virtuous cycle, and it all starts with solid, reliable, and realistic cash projections.

5. Budget Variance Report

How do you connect your projected financials with reality?

A budget variance report examines what you did last month, what you budgeted for, and whether you ran over or under your expected expenditures. It can identify theft or mismanagement, and clue you in to opportunities for improvements and efficiencies.

6. Income Variance Report

Are you making your goals? To know the answer, look to your income variance report.

This report is typically part of your budget variance report; it looks like a profit and loss (P&L) statement set next to your budget. It can help you identify missed goals, problematic conversion rates, and harmful or advantageous trends. Armed with this information, you can hire and fire better, and you can spot opportunities for growth.

That's it! Understand, master, and use *just these six metrics*, and you'll be on your way to increasing your profitability, enjoying more time off, and eliminating the stress and uncertainty crimping your business.

So let's dive in!

#1. Cash Position

Just as in the game of Monopoly, in real business cash is king. How do you measure how much cash your business has at any given moment? How can you use this number to run your operations and guide your planning?

Cash position is really just a measure of how much cash you have. After everything clears the bank—your checks clear, your deposits deposit—what's left?

Do not be deluded into thinking that what the bank says you have at this moment has any bearing on reality. **It is just a snapshot in time** that doesn't take into account other factors.

An example of a check register.

Many entrepreneurs don't track their cash positions accurately. For instance, one of our clients in the oil and gas business used to operate without any bookkeeping systems. They created a good business in a good location, but I realized quickly that they had never learned how to reconcile a checkbook. They rarely wrote down their transactions. So every time they had to write a check, they just logged on to the corporate bank account to see how much money was available and then subtracted out the checks they could remember. This management practice could have led to awful consequences. For instance, what if a big check written to a vendor cleared, draining the account just before payroll went out to 30 employees?

Poor cash position tracking can stimulate financial disorder, employee outrage, loss of vendor services, and even litigation. It's serious stuff!

Here's a related concept to understand: **"the float."**

The float is an artifact of the fact that banks count money twice due to processing delays. As soon as you deposit a check, the bank will credit your account. However, it won't immediately subtract that amount from the account of the person or company who paid you. Until that happens, the check will appear both in your account *and* in the other account.

The float can distort your perception of your cash position and last as long as a week. For instance, let's say you check your business account on your phone and see that you have $12,000 available. So you write an $8,000 check to a vendor, assuming you'll have $4,000 in cash left over afterwards. But then a $6,000 check you wrote to a supplier from last week suddenly clears (thank you, float!). The vendor's check then bounces; he gets mad and cuts off delivery of a critical widget. All of a sudden you're racing to put out fire after fire.

Cash balance is what you have after the float. It may be tough to break out of the habit of checking your bank balance, especially if you're a younger person who has never been exposed to the idea of a check register, or if you're really tight on cash. If you are tight on cash, however, odds are that you have a close eye on your cash position, even if you're not tracking it in a way that's particularly efficient.

Knowing your cash position will give you more confidence. But you still need to know the next piece of the puzzle: *your budget*.

#2. Budget

What is your monthly "nut"? How much does it cost your business every month just to exist?

These questions are huge. It's all well and good to know your cash position, but how long can your business exist without running out of cash? Your *budget* lets you know.

If you haven't budgeted before, you might be a shade embarrassed and also intimidated by the prospect of getting started. Don't be discouraged: even many highly technical and intelligent entrepreneurs don't know how to budget or don't keep one.

You do need to budget, though, because this planning underpins all of your financials. The good news is that the process does not have to be complicated at all.

Here's an example of a **detailed working budget**:

	January	February	March
Ordinary Income/Expense			
Income			
10000 · Income	10,000.00	10,000.00	10,000.00
11000 · Other Income			
Total Income			
Expense			
60000 · Advertising and Promotion	1,500.00	1,500.00	1,500.00
60200 · Automobile Expense	150.00	150.00	150.00
60400 · Bank Service Charges	12.00	12.00	12.00
61400 · Charitable Contributions	0.00	0.00	0.00
61700 · Computer and Internet Expenses	172.00	172.00	172.00
62500 · Dues and Subscriptions	85.00	85.00	85.00
63400 · Interest Expense			
64300 · Meals and Entertainment	200.00	200.00	200.00
64700 · Miscellaneous Expense			
64800 · Office Expense	150.00	150.00	150.00
64900 · Office Supplies	75.00	75.00	75.00
66000 · Payroll Expenses	3,100.00	3,100.00	3,100.00
66500 · Postage and Delivery	100.00	100.00	100.00
66700 · Professional Fees	150.00	150.00	150.00
68000 · Rent	1,200.00	1,200.00	1,200.00
68100 · Telephone Expense	225.00	225.00	225.00
68400 · Travel Expense			
68600 · Utilities	185.00	185.00	185.00
Total Expense	7,304.00	7,304.00	7,304.00
Net Ordinary Income	2,696.00	2,696.00	2,696.00

Not that intimidating, right? ☺

You don't need a 23-page Excel spreadsheet or software beyond QuickBooks. To get started, just go through and estimate your monthly expenses and enter them into your bookkeeping program. If you need help, a bookkeeper or accountant can assist you.

Your budget should be a living, breathing document. It's not something you create once and stash in a drawer, never to look at again. Analyze it and tweak it every month. In the beginning, you won't have precise numbers, so don't be afraid to estimate. Over time, the real world will tell you what to adjust. All numbers in your budget should have a rational basis: make sure they pass the sniff test, and avoid making overly optimistic predictions.

Some entrepreneurs confuse great cash flow with a great budget. One business owner from Florida recently came to us with a budget problem. He had generated $850,000 over one year but somehow still managed to run a $20,000 loss. When he became a client, the first thing we did was look at his expenses. How could he bill and collect so much money and still run at a loss? It turns out that he did have a budget, but it just wasn't appropriate.

He was spending nearly 80% of his gross revenues on payroll (ideally, that number should be 25% to 35%). Once we identified this "budget bloat," he cut back on his staff and consolidated job responsibilities. During the first month after he did this, he ran a $4,000 profit. During the second month, he ran a $12,000 profit.

Such is the pedestrian magic of running your business by a realistic budget!

Your Budget As Scaffolding: Why to Avoid Resisting Structure

Many entrepreneurs, by their constitution, love to improvise and innovate. Structures and procedures seem like nuisances—constraints on creative freedom.

Ironically, though, when you commit a budget to paper, you will actually enjoy more creativity and clarity. This tool lets you know how much money you are spending on what, and what you need to generate to reach key milestones.

You may need an accurate budget to qualify for a loan or other financing, and make smarter hiring and firing decisions. A budget also minimizes risk exposure. For instance, before you spend thousands of dollars on a new website, revamp a huge piece of machinery, or boldly raid a competitor's market, you need to know: *can we comfortably afford this?*

6 Tips for Better Budgeting

1. Avoid Reinventing the Wheel

Use competitive analysis to determine best practices for your industry. What budgeting processes and procedures do your competitors use? What types of software and tools do they use? What typical mistakes do they make with their budgeting, and what are the consequences of those mistakes? What successes and innovations can you copy? Etc.

2. Prepare for a Learning Curve

If you've never budgeted—or if you've budgeted but only in an incomplete and ad-hoc fashion—it may take the process a few months to get into a groove. Don't let that stop you.

3. Be Conservative and Build in Slack

Entrepreneurs have a tendency to get really pumped up about projections of success. Never lose that enthusiasm, but stay grounded by playing with conservative numbers. You might hope that your $200,000-a-year business will blossom and earn $1 million next year, but who knows? If/when your new internet project "goes viral" or you land three high paying clients, you can readjust your budget to reflect those rosy new realities. Right now, make sure the budget is a yardstick of reality, not of a fantasy.

4. Use the Budget to Inform Your Tactics and Strategies

A budget can highlight overspends, and clue you into underutilized resources and potential profit centers. Making mundane improvements, such as slashing your phone bill or leasing out an office to make rent more manageable, can give you breathing room.

5. Keep Your Budget Simple and Current

Some types of budgeting software allow business owners to make complex calculations and projections, but don't miss the forest for the trees. Some tracking is better than none. The real power of this tool isn't just the immediate perspective but rather the *ongoing feedback* it provides about what's working and what's not.

6. Keep the Faith and Stay Grounded

In his bestselling book, *Good to Great*, business author and scholar Jim Collins introduced a concept that he called the "Stockdale Paradox." Named after Admiral Jim Stockdale, who fought in the Vietnam War and wound up tortured in a Vietnamese prison for 8 years, the "Stockdale Paradox" refers to a certain useful mindset about how to forecast outcomes.

Collins asked Stockdale how he survived captivity; the Admiral said he did two things:

First off, he never gave up hope. He held a relentless faith that he would, somehow, survive. Not only would he survive, but he would also turn his captivity into the defining moment of his life. After his release, Stockdale returned home as a hero and later ran for Vice President on Ross Perot's ticket in the 1990s.

Second, he never let optimism carry him away. He told Collins that the people who didn't survive captivity were the "optimists." They would hope that they would get out by Christmas. But Christmas came and went, and they remained in prison. Then they thought they'd leave by Easter. And then Easter came and went without freedom. On and on this went until, per Stockdale, they "died of a broken heart."

The lesson for entrepreneurs is that, when you're budgeting, you want to embrace a dual mentality: be clear and realistic about what's actually going on your business, financially, right now. *Don't lie to yourself.* At the same time, *maintain faith that your business will succeed*, by hook or by crook, even if revenues are down or sales have plummeted.

Beyond Budgeting

You may have the greatest budget in the world and an appropriately optimistic/realistic plan to march forward. But you still need to bring cash into the business. To that end, let's turn next to our next crucial (and surprisingly misunderstood) number: *Accounts Receivable*.

#3. Accounts Receivable (A/R)

Whether you're running a service business, such as a law firm or a doctor's office, or you sell software or hard goods, you need to track and manage ***accounts receivable***.

Most entrepreneurs—particularly business owners in the service industry—don't really understand how A/R should be handled. I have seen business owners stand up and brag that they have almost half a million dollars in A/R. Some of these owners think of A/R as a measure of profitability—a prestige indicator of how much work they've produced. For instance, let's say you billed $500,000 to a customer and collected $50,000 on that account. That means you still have $450,000 to collect. You might treat that $450,000 as a kind of "rainy day" fund or even a savings account.

Many entrepreneurs don't sweat the prospect of collecting this money, because they operate by a moral code, and they assume that others share that vision. If you provided a service or a product, and the customer appreciated the work and got value from it, the law of reciprocity should dictate that the customer show appreciation by paying the balance owed.

When I really need the money, you imagine, *the delinquent client will pay me because I helped him.*

The subconscious assumption is that A/R is almost like "emergency cash" that you don't have to declare to the IRS—a secret invisible stash the government can't see!

Not so fast. It's not actually unrecognized income.

It is a loan.

Out of your pocket.

At zero interest.

I realize that this sounds harsh, but it is the reality. Here's something to think about along those lines. Do you use credit cards? Do you ever carry balances on your cards? I did when I started my business, even though I'm a financial advisor. Sometimes to support the growth of a business, you can (and should) finance using credit cards. But if you have A/R outstanding to collect—and you're simultaneously carrying a balance on your cards—you've actually just made an unsecured loan at zero interest to your clients that's costing you anywhere from 18% to 29%, depending on the rate of your card!

In other words, it costs you 18% to 29% to offer the privilege of lending money to delinquent clients so they can take their families on vacation.

That's really nice of you.

Even if you understand, intellectually, that this arrangement is not ideal—that you should not provide unsecured loans in this fashion—you may not be that convinced that improving your A/R processes should be a priority.

Maybe you believe that the details of A/R will "work themselves out," once you get your marketing and sales machines operating better. *One or two delinquent accounts won't bring the house down, if we bring in more business.* Or maybe collecting A/R has not (yet!) been an issue for your business, so you believe you can safely ignore this number for now.

Here's the issue, though. If you fail to adopt effective A/R "hygiene" during your current stage of business growth and development, when will you?

As Sir Arthur Doyle sagely noted in *The Memoirs of Sherlock Holmes*: "It has long been an axiom of mine that the little things are infinitely the most important."

You might shrug off A/R losses as only a sacrifice of your time, but that's inaccurate. You pay costs to provide services or sell products, no matter what business you run. Many service businesses, for instance, operate on what's known as the Rule of Thirds:

- One-third of money billed goes to the person who does the work;
- One-third goes to overhead (rent, computers, office supplies, etc.); and
- One-third goes to the owners and to profit.

Bearing that in mind, let's say you billed John Doe $15,000 for some customized software you built for him, but he hasn't yet paid you. Writing that code for John Doe, on the other hand, **cost your business $10,000**. You paid your team $5,000 to help John, and you also paid for the overhead necessary to do the work for him.

In addition to the cash costs, sloppy A/R practices lead to deeper, hidden costs: *opportunity costs*. In other words, what could you have done with your time/business resources—instead of working on John's project—to grow your company? What cool contingency or R&D projects did you decline because John's project booked up your calendar or because you had too much money/resources tied up in John's account?

- Maybe you could have purchased an ad that would have generated three new clients.
- Maybe you could have hired a new developer to create a better social media site for your marquis product.
- Maybe you could have taken off time to reconnect with your family and/or give your employees needed down time before a new surge of business.
- Maybe you could have spent resources to tighten your policies and procedures to automate several chronically annoying tasks.

Identifying opportunity costs is hard work, because thinking about "what you might have done" with your time and resources does not come naturally for most people. In the famous detective story *Silver Blaze,* Sherlock Holmes solves a crime with an astute deduction. He realizes that a guard dog that should have barked during the night in question didn't bark and thus concludes that the dog must have known the criminal suspect.

Holmes used a kind of reasoning known as *counterfactual thinking* to identify the dog that didn't bark. Our minds are excellent pattern seekers, but they're generally not very good at looking for what's not there—for understanding the true costs of missed opportunities.

The point is that when you don't track A/R correctly you may not see the consequences immediately. But if you DO adopt better financial habits, you'll hedge better against negative events and be better positioned to take advantage of serendipities—accidental good fortune.

Take A/R seriously. If you give a delinquent client a free loan that costs you 29% to service, what are you giving up in terms of missed opportunities?

One last thing: badgering delinquent clients can sour the mood of everyone in your business.

So what's the solution?

Here's the basic idea: *establish excellent A/R protocol right out of the gate.*

If you sell services, spell out your A/R policy during the initial consultation. If you sell products on installment plans, follow the same approach: educate customers about how you collect money at the point of sale. Preemptively teach your customers how to be good customers.

Here's a real world example. I have a client who's a divorce attorney in Florida; he works on high-end divorces. When he first called me, and we discussed the problems in his business, he told me that he didn't have time to obtain new clients, because he was always calling existing clients, badgering them to pay for work he had completed for them.

He had a fee agreement retainer, but this retainer was far too low. He asked for $5,000 up front, but his average divorce billed out at $50,000. Some of his cases exceeded six figures. So first things first, we changed the retainer so he could collect more cash up front.

Then I asked about his evergreen clause, the paragraph in an attorney's fee agreement that requires the client to keep a retainer of a certain amount on deposit with the attorney until the case is completed. He had one but never enforced it, making it an irrelevant detail. He took people's credit cards but didn't put their credit card information in the fee agreement. He had no authorization form that allowed him to charge a client's card automatically on the 10th of the month. Nor did he tell his clients that he would stop work if/when their trust accounts went dry.

We made several adjustments. We added a credit card authorization form and added language to his fee agreement authorizing him to charge the client's card the amount due on the 10th of the month. He also started telling clients that, if/when their trust accounts ran out of money, and if the credit card was declined, he would stop work. The client would then have a chance to fix things; if the client didn't, he would withdraw from the case.

We created this very simple, front-end process for his A/R. He set expectations. He taught his clients how to be good clients. And he enforced this system. He "magically" now has a lot more money and much more time. On the 10th of the month, his bookkeeper goes through and charges all of his clients' cards the appropriate amount. If a card fails to go through, the bookkeeper calls the client to see if there is a problem, such as theft or fraud. The next week, the bookkeeper sits down with the attorney, reviews the balances in the trust and tells him whose card was declined and who hasn't paid.

He still makes follow-up calls for A/R, but instead of having to make an arduous 30 calls a month, he only has to make three or four.

Fine-tuning your A/R process may not seem like the sexiest part of running a business. You might love product development and want to spend your time testing new gadgets or chatting with engineers. Or you may be obsessed with marketing and managing your brand. But establishing a good A/R process is important. You can remove a big constraint that could be choking your business in ways that you may not even recognize until after you fix things.

A/R is created the very first time you meet with your client or do business with your customer. Here's what you need to be examining on a monthly basis:

- How much has the business loaned out?
- How much can the business collect in the next week?
- How much can the business collect in next two months?
- What should you do with the rest of the money in Accounts Receivable? Should you go to collections or write it off? Should you cross your fingers and hope that the client or customer will come to his senses and pay you?

A/R is like rotting fruit. Every day that goes by, you're less likely to collect it. By the time you've hit 90 days, you'll be lucky to collect about 10% of what you're owed.

A good, solid collection rate for A/R is 90% to 95%. During your initial conversation with your clients, when you establish A/R expectations, go over the following:

- **Discuss your fee agreement, retainer, and billing practices;**

- **Obtain credit card authorization** (if your business does not take credit cards, strongly consider amending your process, so you can!); and

- **Clearly define your stop work policy.** (Obviously, you don't want to stop work to the detriment of your license or other credentials.)

When you include credit cards in your payment arrangements, you let your clients or customers pay the interest. Get retainers. Get credit card numbers and authorizations to charge. Stop work when clients run out of money. And collect your money, so you don't end up with a year's salary tied up in A/R.

A/R flows naturally into *cash projections* – the next number we need to cover.

#4. Cash Projections

Let's do a mini-review:

1. You've figured out your *cash position*, so you now know exactly how much cash you have in the bank, after you account for all outstanding credits and debits.

2. You've done your *budget*, so you know how long that cash will last.

3. You've got a handle on your *accounts receivable*, so you know how much cash should be flowing into your business and from what sources.

So far, so good! See? This isn't that complicated ☺

Your next mission—should you choose to accept it—is to use the information you've generated to create *cash projections*, also known as **cash flow forecasts**.

Calculating this number does not have to be complicated. **It's not rocket science.** The goal is to create an outlook, so you can see forward six to eight weeks. Depending on the nature of your business, you might want to do this projection by week, so you can really measure the business's pulse and make course corrections if need be.

I keep a really simple spreadsheet with about 8 lines that I give my clients to use. This works. The sheet is easy to manage and provides tons of information. It covers major categories, such as recurring weekly expenses, payroll, income, and your starting cash balance.

Here's an example of a cash flow forecast template:

Week Beginning	Date	Date	Date	Date
Beginning Balance*:		$0	$0	$0
Regular Bills				
Payroll*				
Extraordinary Expenses				
LOC Drawdown				
Deposits**	Income Est	Income Est	Income Est	Income Est
Ending Balance	$0	$0	$0	$0
Cash Available***	$50,000	$50,000	$50,000	$50,000
LOC Balance	$0	$0	$0	$0
* Please double check and edit this amount every Monday ** Enter as deposits are made. Estimates based on XXXXXX *** Based on $50,000 LOC				

If you're interested in using this template and filling in the blanks for your own business, direct your browser here: www.capcath.com/forms.

To bring financial clarity to your business, call Cathedral Capital, Inc. at 817.338.1011

So **how is this number useful**? What does this forecast accomplish for your business?

Let's take a look at a real world example to illustrate its utility. I have a client in Portland, and we were going through his numbers the second week in January. As I examined his cash flow forecast, I saw that he was due to have a cash crunch the week of March 17.

After he hyperventilated for a few seconds, we started talking about how to manage this crisis. In his case, he did not have A/R as an option, because he had set up his A/R systems as we discussed in Chapter 3. In other words, he collected his payments on time, so he didn't have an A/R "savings account."

We brainstormed and came up with other ways he could boost his income. When I spoke with him three weeks later, he elatedly reported that he no longer had a cash crunch in March.

How were we able to overcome this obstacle so easily?

We knew *two months ahead* about the crisis looming on the horizon, so we had plenty of time to solve the problem before it exploded. Had this client *lacked* effective financial controls, he would have checked his bank balance on March 14 and discovered, much to his dismay, that he would not make payroll on the 20th. With a just a week's notice, he would have had almost no lead time to solve the problem. It would be like strapping on your seatbelt after your car has already started to skid out of control—not very effective!

Perhaps he could have pulled off a miracle by borrowing from his personal finances or begging his employees to wait on their checks for two weeks. But even if he did avert the crisis without crashing and burning, he would have endured a harrowing few weeks, and he'd be left flat-footed to respond to other crises or opportunities.

Cash-related course corrections are always easier to do when you see them from far away.

NASA has a program that scans the sky for potential asteroids that might be on a collision course with Earth. Our space engineers need to identify and track these large chunks of rock and ice, because if a big one collides with us, we could be wiped out, much like the dinosaurs met their maker 65 million years ago when a space rock hit the Earth, leaving the gigantic Chicxulub Crater to scar the Gulf of Mexico.

We stay on red alert for these types of impacts to protect Earth. We need good detection systems. If we can spot an asteroid that's on a collision course with us 15 years from now, we can send a small probe to nudge it off course with little more than a kiss to perturb its orbit. However, if we don't discover the problem until a week or two prior to impact, there is nothing we can do to alter the course of that asteroid.

Okay, when I said cash projections weren't "rocket science" earlier, maybe I lied!

The point is that that your cash projections act in many ways like NASA's asteroid detection systems. They serve as sensitive detectors to alert you to potential danger (and sometimes opportunity), so that you can **maneuver at a relatively leisurely pace to avoid calamity.**

What if your business is incredibly stable?

Well, it might look stable based on your current information and forecast. *But you never know.* No matter how solid your business and market appear to be, surprises are always in the offing. Author and speaker, David Allen, whom Fast Company once called the "personal productivity guru," wrote about this high-level business concept in his bestselling book *Ready for Anything*. This quote is well worth pondering, if you're looking for reasons to justify engaging in regular cash flow forecasts:

> Something is coming – probably within a few days – that is going to change your world. You don't see it yet. You don't know what it's about. But it's there, rolling inexorably forward, destined to throw you a curve that you do not expect. It could show up sooner or later – but it *will* show up. Trust me.
>
> Write down these words exactly four weeks from today in your calendar: 'David Allen said a month ago that something was coming I couldn't foresee that would affect me significantly.' Prove me wrong. Are you ready? Is that unexpected event or input going to add insult or injury by making you feel more out of control? Or are you going to see it as the next creative opportunity that takes you to a new level of expression and contribution? How are you preparing for the surprises that the new experience will invariably throw your way?

Hopefully, you get the point: you need to do cash projections and to consult them regularly (like my clients and I do), so you can deflect the metaphorical "meteors" headed towards your business, and also to grab opportunities that your more myopic competitors will miss.

So how do you crunch this number? **What are the nuts and bolts?**

In the short term, **look at the A/R** that you expect to come in for the current month. For the next month, you should also be tracking your **Work In Progress (WIP).** I check this every week. Are you doing enough work this month to fund next month's operations? You should also **know your budget** and **know your collection rate** during the first 30 days, so you can tell, easily, when you cross the threshold into profitability.

Remember: the average successful business has a billing collection rate of 90% to 95%. When I started working with a law firm a few years ago, I crunched the numbers and found that the firm's collection rate had fallen below 80%. That was not ideal. It's kind of like this: imagine you're running a car dealership, and every fifth person who walks in the door gets a car for free. You can't run a business like that! But we had to be realistic and accept that, for the time being, our collection rate would only be 80% while we improved our systems and processes.

One key rule of running a successful business is "never lie to yourself." You can (and should) be excited about your business, but you must also learn to operate in reality. The six numbers that you're learning can give you the guy wires you need to keep sober control of the helm.

In any event, let's say you have a 30-day collection rate of 90% and a monthly nut of about $50,000. The day that your WIP gets to about $55,000, you've covered your expenses for the next month. Everything after that is ***profit for you***.

Alternatively, let's say you're over half way through the month. You're concerned because your collection rate is not high. You only have $20,000 in billable WIP. You have some big decisions to make. You could pull your team off R&D or off of slow paying clients to work on accounts that might pay faster or sooner. You could push lower paying or more labor-intensive work off by a few weeks. Get creative, and solve the cash crunch.

After you triage (if you need to triage), turn your attention to the longer term. Examine your marketing efforts and the capacity of your factory to generate business. If you can't project out that capacity, you will likely face periodic cash crunches at random intervals. This can make life quite unpleasant, to say the least.

Here's how you figure out capacity. Your company presumably uses employees and possibly outsourcers to complete its work. Let's assume that these employees and/or contractors work on an hourly billing rate. If so, each person should have an hourly billing goal. Multiply the billing rate by the monthly goal for each person, and then sum up those amounts to get a number. That number is what your business is capable of producing every month, through its employees. This is also known as capacity. For instance:

- 2 part-time developers whom you bill at $120/hour times 100 hours/month $12,000
- 3 software editors whom you bill at $80/hour times 400 hours/month $32,000
- 1 client liaison whom you bill at $150/hour times 60 hours/month $ 9,000

TOTAL   **$63,000**

This number is based on **two assumptions**:

1. You assume that your employees will **meet their billable hour goals**.

2. You assume that **you will have enough work** to keep your team busy.

If your people are doing all the work they have available to them, but you're still not hitting your billing goals, your people should not be blamed. Your rainmakers need to step up!

If you don't have enough work in the pipeline, you need to get more. That's obvious, right? The point of doing cash projections is that you can identify precisely what you need, when, and why. You can then strategize and come up with fun ways to fill your pipeline. If you're facing this problem right now, **try this little exercise to achieve immediate clarity.**

Working by yourself (or with your executive team), complete 20 distinct answers to the following sentence: *"We can generate more work in our pipeline by _____"*

1. _____
2. _____
3. _____
4. _____
5. _____
6. _____
7. _____
8. _____
9. _____
10. _____
11. _____
12. _____
13. _____
14. _____
15. _____
16. _____
17. _____
18. _____
19. _____
20. _____

Be sure to enumerate at least 20 possibilities. Often, the best brainstorming moments happen late in this process, after you've generated the first 10 to 15 ideas from top of mind.

Here's another way to generate possibilities. Ask the following questions (and try to give 20 answers to each of them):

- "If we wanted to generate 10 times the amount of work we currently need to feed our pipeline, we would _____."

- "If we wanted to generate the work we need to feed our pipeline 10 times faster than we actually do, we would _____."

Don't worry about constraining your thinking when you brainstorm. You can go back later and sort the wheat from the chaff. The point of these exercises is to stretch your mind and expand your creative thinking. The cash projections constrain your thinking and give you clear benchmarks to hit, which you can use as a springboard for better planning.

Here's an example of how to apply these concepts.

I have a client in McKinney, Texas, who gets three to four new clients every time he gives a speech. When we go through his cash flow forecasts every month, I find out how many speeches he has scheduled. If that number is insufficient to generate the revenue we need, I send him out to beat the bushes and find more speaking opportunities. It's just that simple.

Track your conversation rates, and be honest and realistic about what's happening.

For instance, let's say you run a service business. You know that 20 potential customers will find your website and call your office every month. Of those who call, 14 will make an appointment. Of those 14, 12 will actually show up. Of the 12 who show up, 6 will retain your business and hire you to do work. That's a conversation rate of approximately 30%.

That may not seem wonderful. Statistically, however, that's a very solid conversation rate. If you're not counting how many calls you get, how many no shows, and how many last-minute non-deciders, you might have a falsely high conversation rate. For instance, your conversation rate may *seem* to hover around 60%, when it's actually 30%.

Track every step of the process, and seek to identify your true constraint:

- Maybe you're not bringing enough new prospects into the business.
- Maybe your web marketing is driving people away or sending you the wrong people.
- Maybe your sales team isn't putting the right offers in front of people.

What's the bottleneck in your conversation process? By tracking what's happening at each step, you can make smart adjustments to your plan.

Let's say you give three speeches a month, each of which generates three new clients on average, each of whom is worth about $3,000 in business. Each account lasts 30 days on average. That means that, if you do three speeches, you should generate $27,000, which you can collect within 30 days. Not bad!

Ask these questions to get a handle on your conversations and the possible bottlenecks:

- **What's the average customer lifetime?** Once a client starts to buy your products or services, how long does he stay with you?

- **What's the average value of your customer?** Finding this is easy. Just add up the revenue generated by all your customers and divide it by the number of customers.

- **How many prospects do you need to get a single conversation?**

- **What's the length of time** between someone becoming a prospect and someone becoming a paying client?

- **What does it cost you,** in terms of time, money, and resources, to make your phone ring or grow your lead list?

Armed with this information, you can work backwards through time to figure out what you need to do to make the numbers work. Simply plug this information into a spreadsheet. If you know that, every time you engage in X marketing tactic, you generate Y referrals worth Z dollars each, you will know how many times you need to do X to make your cash projections work.

When you do this number right, business actually becomes fun, like a game. But unlike winning a game of Monopoly or Scrabble, which only gives you "bragging rights," winning at business should mean profits for everyone the business touches: yourself, your clients, your family, and your employees. It's like an episode of *Oprah*: everyone wins!

Cash flow is interesting, because it's a weekly budget. **Weekly projections help prevent weekly crises**. For instance, your budget might tell you that you need $60,000 to run every month, because that's your nut. But you also need to *get more granular* to make sure your inflows and outflows match up.

I have a client who has a big Fortune 500 company as his client. That big client has a 90-day pay cycle. So when my client bills on January 1st, he doesn't get paid until April 1st. That's a long time. In the interim, he must finance his company for three months. To make sure he can run the engine, he needs an accurate cash flow forecast.

In general, especially for service businesses, the first and third weeks tend to be tough. From the 28th of the month to the 5th of the next month, bills, rent, and payroll generally all hit at the same time. The 16th of the month can also be "crunch time" because you need to make payroll again. Service businesses generally bill clients on a net 30. You bill on the 1st, and the clients pay you on the 28th, for instance.

You can use your cash flow forecast to figure out when you should pay your bills. *Do we pay now or hold off?* Make adjustments to make life easier. You might consider changing the due date for your credit card bill from the 16th—when you're slammed by payroll—to the 29th, after you've started to receive that month's checks.

To manage cash flow, you may need to be able to annualize in this fashion. The money you bring in at the end of the month can help fund next month's operations.

I like my monthly clients to have access to at least three months of operating expenses, as a mix of cash and a line of credit. You don't necessarily need three months of cash in the bank. In fact, hoarding or stockpiling cash can cost you money, because you're not putting that money to work most efficiently. Ultimately, you need to figure out how much cash you need in reserve based on your type of business, your market, your personal risk tolerance, etc. One of my clients gets twitchy if he doesn't have a whole year of cash in hand!

Other people hold cash for different reasons. Billionaire Warren Buffet, for instance, keeps cash as a war chest; he wants to be liquid enough to pounce on opportunities that seem appropriate. He foregoes income now by holding his cash in reserve, knowing that he will find a way to generate a higher return on it at a later date.

#5. Budget Variance Report

The *budget variance report* is useful, because it allows you to see how well your projections match up to reality. You've invested hard work into anticipating your business's financials. But did you project correctly? If so, what can that tell you? If not, what can that tell you?

You can use practically any accounting software system to prepare this report, which shows you what you did last month, what you budgeted for last month, and whether you were over or under your expected expenditures.

Here's an example, building off the budget we created in Chapter 2:

	January	Budget	$ Over Budget	% of Budget	Feb 14
Ordinary Income/Expense					
Income					
10000 · Income	8,625.00	10,000.00	-1,375.00	86.25%	8,7
11000 · Other Income	981.44		981.44	100.0%	971.
Total Income	9,606.44	10,000.00	-393.56		9,691.1
Expense					
60000 · Advertising and Promotion	2,344.27	1,500.00	844.27	156.29%	4,050.54
60200 · Automobile Expense	65.05	150.00	-84.95	43.37%	518.1
60400 · Bank Service Charges	5.00	12.00	-7.00	41.67%	0.00
61400 · Charitable Contributions	0.00	0.00	0.00	0.0%	320.0
61700 · Computer and Internet Expenses	10.61	172.00	-161.39	6.17%	9
62500 · Dues and Subscriptions	0.00	85.00	-85.00	0.0%	0.
63400 · Interest Expense	0.00		0.00	0.0%	
64300 · Meals and Entertainment	0.00	200.00	-200.00	0.0%	
64700 · Miscellaneous Expense	0.00		0.00	0.0%	0.00
64800 · Office Expense	376.85	150.00	226.85	251.23%	517.43
64900 · Office Supplies	669.31	75.00	594.31	892.41%	238.5
66000 · Payroll Expenses	4,626.01	3,100.00	1,526.01	149.23%	4,61
66500 · Postage and Delivery	180.07	100.00	80.07	180.07%	0.00
66700 · Professional Fees	0.00	150.00	-150.00	0.0%	
68000 · Rent	1,200.00	1,200.00	0.00	100.0%	1,200.0
68100 · Telephone Expense	134.09	225.00	-90.91	59.6%	134.3
68400 · Travel Expense	0.00		0.00	0.0%	853.4
68600 · Utilities	46.75	185.00	-138.25	25.27%	49
Total Expense	9,658.01	7,304.00	2,354.01	132.23%	12,6
Net Ordinary Income	-51.57	2,696.00	-2,747.57	-1.91%	

This report will tell you the percentage that you were over/under your budget as well as the dollar amount that you were over/under. Go through each item, line item by line item, and make decisions based on these facts. Did you go over for a good reason or for a bad reason?

When you notice discrepancies, generate hypotheses:

- Did mismanagement play a roll?

- Did an employee or vendor steal from the company?

- Did your accountant accidentally pay rent twice because of sloppy bookkeeping?

Here's a dramatic story to illustrate how the budget variance report can shine a light on lurking business dangers. A friend was in South Carolina giving a speech, and he struck up a conversation with a man who owned a limo company. They discussed the numbers of this business, and the limo company owner gushed over how much he loved his budget variance report. Here's why. One month, after preparing this report, he discovered a minor but annoying glitch. For some reason, he was way over on his fuel budget. So he investigated. He had issued each driver a company credit card to purchase gas. Most of the drivers' bills were normal. But one driver had a really big bill—way more than what it should have been.

So the limo company owner and his team examined the individual charges and discovered that this driver had been fueling up to the tune of 35 to 40 gallons every time. But his car only held 18 gallons! Red flag. The owner called the gas station, which let him watch security tapes of his driver filling up. Once he finished, he pulled forward. His wife then pulled in behind him and topped off her tank. Then a neighbor came and did the same.

Obviously, that was end of that driver's career with the company!

But think about how profound that "catch" was. What if the limo owner *hadn't* done a budget variance report and hadn't realized that one of his drivers was siphoning 20 gallons of fuel every fuel up? Frankly, the scam could have gone under the radar for months, if not years. Over time, the theft could have added up to thousands of dollars. Even more importantly, had the owner not caught the culprit, he might still be working for the company.

Who knows what other unethical or even downright illegal activities he could have done? Would he have ripped off clients? Would he have encouraged other drivers to pull the same scam? The old saying that "a rotten apple spoils the bunch" is not far from reality. It only takes one or two problematic employees or outsourcers to wreak devastation on a business. The cascading repercussions of wrongdoing can undermine what you're trying to do in subtle but real ways. Business, like baseball, is a game of inches. You need to be able to identify seemingly "small" problems—like a limo driver consuming more than his fair share of fuel—because mismanagement or theft is often the tip of a much larger iceberg.

Of course, being over or under budget doesn't always indicate a calamity or even a problem.

For instance, maybe you bought more office supplies than expected because you just landed a marquis client. You splurged on a whole bunch of notebooks, binders, and colored ink to put together a marketing presentation to win that business.

No problem. With this report in hand, you can determine why you were over (or under) budget. It's also not always bad for projections to be inaccurate. In fact, I love when my clients are over budget on certain items—for instance, credit card merchant fees. Why? If they're over on these fees, it means that more people are walking in the door and becoming clients or customers. Their collection rate is probably going up. They're generating money faster, because they're automatically charging more clients on the 10th of the month, as opposed to waiting for them to mail a check in on the 25th.

The budget variance report is only a tool: you still need to interpret it strategically. But over time, as it becomes more familiar, it can help you micromanage (in a good way) your business, spot trends, and adjust as necessary.

Have you been overspending in a particular category for three months in a row? If so, perhaps it's time to adjust your budget or change what you're spending on that line item. Your budget will change. It's a living, breathing thing. Every month, you will get feedback, which you can use to adjust your course of action.

Here's nice metaphor to solidify this idea. If you're a photography buff, you know that dozens of factors can affect an image's quality and clarity. These factors might include your filters, your lenses, the number of pixels available, if you use a digital instrument, etc. Blurry images are usually less valuable than crisper ones. If police want to catch a criminal that just robbed a convenience store, they'd prefer a picture that shows every last whisker on the thief's face, not an inscrutably blurry image that narrows the suspect down to 10 million people.

The budget variance report provides a similar kind of clarity in your business.

You can see, line item by line item, what's going wrong (or what's going right), deduce why, and take needed actions. On some level, it's almost ridiculous that business owners do not all track this report. Would you ever fly on a plane flown by a pilot who never looked at the dashboard and instead just "flew by feel"? Of course not! Yet for some reason, many entrepreneurs "fly blindly" in a similar sense when they run their businesses.

Your budget variance report will allow you to run your business more strategically with less effort, and it will greatly simplify your planning tasks.

#6. Income Variance Report

In addition to understanding your business in a granular sense—which you can do using the 6 tools we are discussing—you also want to understand the broad sweep of things.

What's happening over the long-term in your business?

Let's take an extreme example. Say you're running a fireworks business. The fireworks industry is closely regulated, and you may only be allowed to sell fireworks within a window of about 21 days during fireworks season, leading up to the 4th of July. If you run such a business, you will have *just six weeks* to pace up for the frenzied season—to purchase inventory, train staff, market like crazy, and sell your fireworks. Then the season ends, and your business needs to coast again until Christmas season, when the next window opens and you need to surge your business for New Year's Eve.

If your business operates in this spiky fashion—and almost all businesses do, to some extent—you can miss important variations if you're too nose deep in the short-term numbers. A year-to-date *income variance report* lets you see the forest for the trees.

Consider the retail industry as another example. During Easter, Christmas, and other holidays, retail experiences a so-called "seasonality of expenses." Variations are normal. You must graph and track your variations, so that you know what's acceptable for your business.

Many service firms actually have it easy. They don't have perishables to stock and track. There is no big inventory of products that could "rot on the vine," nor a fleet of vehicles that must be maintained and fueled up just in case. Service firms may only need a phone, a computer, and some other basic office tools.

But you still need to look past the weekly variations and even past the monthly variations. If trends look down, consider cutting staff or slashing other expenses so you don't wind up out of money and having to fire people at the last minute or, even worse, coming home to your family without any money to buy groceries. You need to know where you stand.

Nuts and Bolts of the Income Variance Report

Your income variance report is part of your budget variance report. It looks like a profit and loss statement set next to your budget.

Remember earlier, when we derived your budget? We discussed two key assumptions:

1. All of your people will meet their billing goals.

2. You will have enough work in the pipeline to meet your goals.

Let's dive a little deeper into assumption #1. I have a client in Pennsylvania who hired a new employee last fall. She used her income variance report to determine whether she could finance this new hire. The woman's salary was relatively expensive, but based on our projections, the employee's billing should have paid for herself in about two weeks. However, the first month after this new recruit began working, I looked at my client's revenues and found that they were lower than we had expected. So I dug in and started identifying who produced what.

It turns out that the new hire had been under-producing. I instructed my client to have a discussion with her to ensure that the recruit's 35 hours brought in enough revenue to justify her position. However, the next month, my client had a similar problem. This time, I sent my client to her Human Resources director, who coached her about how to motivate the recruit to produce the needed revenue numbers. She got the message across. My client had the right conversations, and now the new recruit is hitting her goals. We built a model that required the hire to hit certain targets, and it worked.

The income variance report helps you **identify problems and see solutions** that you might not otherwise see. For instance, you might spot a spike in income over a few months; you can then track down what caused that spike and figure out how to replicate it, if possible.

One golden rule of entrepreneurship is "do what works." If you have proof that something is working in your business—causing revenue to spike, for instance—by all means, do that "thing" again. Replicate it. Scale it.

The P&L report highlights where your company is doing well and where you have room to grow. Investors can also use a P&L report to determine the health and wellbeing of your business if/when you want to sell it.

Generally, this report consists of two sections.

Section #1 covers revenue. This section catalogs all your gains, such as income from selling services or products, revenue generated from bank interest, etc.

Some questions you may want to ask include:

- Are our projections correct?
- Are we really accomplishing what we want to achieve?
- Can we identify glaring (or even subtle) indicators of theft or mismanagement?
- Are our sales people working?
- Is our income acceptable?
- Does our spending exceed our budget?
- Are we buying gas for our employees' friends, or is it just costing us more to run the business than we anticipated?

Section #2, which covers expenses, includes labor costs, materials, and depreciation.

As you assess the revenue component, look at sales, because sales efforts should be predictable and *repeatable*. You might have generated income from a random source that you can't repeat. That's nice. But if you can't repeat it or scale it, what good does it do you? Not much.

Look at sales for individual services or products as line items to determine what's really cooking and what campaigns have gone off the rails, so that you can attend to them strategically. Ideally, **revenue should go up** in between each P&L report.

Examine **net sales** as well. This figure includes the sales that you generate operationally as well as extraordinary gains. For instance, maybe you sold a big piece of equipment and generated $30,000. That's great, but you need to catalog that sale separately, so it doesn't misinform your assumptions about what the future should hold.

In terms of expenses, you need to **track the costs of direct labor**, such as your COO and your receptionist. (This figure doesn't include sales or office staff, since the more you produce, the more those costs rise.)

You also need to **track operating costs**, such as rent, depreciation of company assets, salary costs, interest on loans, legal fees, etc. You can use different financial metrics to give you more information, including gross profit, operating profit, and net profit.

- To get **gross profit**, just subtract the cost of goods from your revenue. This helps you determine the efficiency of your business, and it's a useful number for identifying sales quotas in the future and establishing your prices.

- To determine **operating profit**, subtract operating expenses from gross profit. Operating profit is also known as EBIT ("earnings before tax and interest").

- Your **net profit** is your operating profit minus other expenses, such as taxes you owe and interest on credit cards.

With these ratios in hand, you can use your income variance report to make better forecasting decisions and increase your level of clarity and control over all business operations.

#7. The Balance Sheet

This is a "bonus" number that may be useful for small business owners; it's a powerful tool for entrepreneurs who are already earning substantial annual revenue.

Here is what's on the ***balance sheet***:

1. **Your assets**—the things your business owns. These items might include your bank account, your furniture, your computers, etc.

2. **Your liabilities**—the things your business owes. For instance, maybe you took out a line of credit to pay for your office furniture.

3. **Your equity**—This is the net worth of your company. It's a measure of the things you own minus the things you owe. Ideally, this should be a positive number!

When we take on new clients, the first thing I examine is the balance sheet. Within seconds of looking at this gauge, I can tell whether a business is in trouble or healthy.

This report identifies your financial position at a certain point in time. It allows creditors, investors, managers, suppliers, and competitors to suss out what's happening inside the business. Your balance sheet can determine whether you can secure a loan or pique investor interest in buying your business.

Let's take a look at these three fields—assets, liabilities, and equity—in slightly more detail.

Assets include what the business owns. This can be a diverse catalog of "stuff." For instance, you may have documented policies and procedures. Those are useful. They add value to your company. An investor pondering whether to buy your business might be enticed if he sees that you've meticulously documented and systematized key aspects of your marketing and sales, for instance. Conversely, if you have accounts receivable waiting (potentially!) for you to collect, you may have a hard time convincing a buyer that your A/R has value.

Other assets might include:

- Cash on hand;
- Any buildings or property the business owns;
- Equipment;
- Costs you've paid in advance, such as insurance, ad spends, legal bills, and inventory; and
- Improvements you've made to the property.

The items on the balance sheet might be classified into groups, such as your current assets, your investments, building and equipment, intangibles, etc.

Liabilities, meanwhile, are what the company owes to creditors. For instance, maybe your business owes $40,000 to a vendor. Or maybe an injured employee sued you and won a judgment against your business for $200,000.

Different liabilities might include:

- Income taxes you owe;
- Accounts payable;
- Salaries that you owe your employees, contractors and freelancers; and
- Interest that you owe on credit cards and other accounts.

Liabilities might be sub-classified as long-term payables versus current payables.

To determine **equity,** simply subtract liabilities from assets. If your business is a sole proprietorship, this is known as owner's equity. If you own a corporation, this number will be known as stockholders equity. But it really describes the same basic concept—this is the value of your company.

The balance sheet offers a truly global picture of what's happening in your business at a particular time by highlighting its key capabilities and weaknesses.

Conclusion

Take a deep long breath and let it go – you've done it!

You have now identified and understood the six key concepts that you need to know to manage the core financials of your business. Hopefully, this process wasn't too overwhelming. And hopefully you will start tracking and managing by these numbers as soon as possible to improve how you do things, become more profitable, slash unnecessary expenses, and increase your ability to fulfill your mission and serve the world.

Most financial advice for business owners is much too technical; it contains extraneous details that can leave entrepreneurs feeling overwhelmed and incompetent. It takes guts, commitment, and sweat to get a business off the ground and keep it running. If you don't have a finance or accounting background, the thought of learning, metabolizing, and implementing 50 different financial reports might seem ridiculous—for understandable reasons.

Obviously, educated business owners know that they must track their financials. But when it all seems so complicated and mysterious, it's easy to throw up your hands and say "Not now! I will get to this later." That would be fine, except that "later" never seems to arrive.

You can drive your business "blind" to your financials and possibly get away with it for a little while. But just like it's not a great idea to hurtle down the freeway at 80 miles per hour while wearing a blindfold, it's also not wise to operate while financially blind. Sooner or later, you WILL hit an obstacle and hurt yourself and possibly others in the process.

This book has really been a manifesto of sorts for small business owners and entrepreneurs, as much as it has been a teaching tool. I want you to understand that tracking and using your financials does not have to be complicated. You can do this!

Once you start running your business using these six numbers (or seven, if you want to throw in the balance sheet), you will enjoy so much more control and clarity, you won't even believe it. The tracking will create a virtuous cycle in your business that will boost your marketing, finesse your sales, improve how you relate to your employees, outsourcers, and clients, fine tune your factory, and create better systems and processes.

By **tracking your cash position**, you'll know exactly how much you have in your accounts, so you don't accidentally suffer a payroll crisis that sends your staff into mutiny.

By **tracking your budget**, you'll know exactly what it costs to keep your business up and running. You can identify, for instance, whether you're paying way too much for an outsourcer or whether your salary is too low—and take corrective action ASAP.

By **tracking your accounts receivable** more effectively, you'll avoid doing silly things like providing a delinquent client with a zero interest loan to finance a holiday, while you pay 29% interest on your credit card bill.

By **tracking your cash projections**, you'll catch bookkeeper mishaps and stop dubious employees from stealing from your business. Catching such "little problems" before they blossom into "big ones" is powerful; it can ensure that the right people are doing the right things in your business and that the wrong people are ejected before they cause harm.

By **tracking your budget variance report**, you can see how and where your financial plans diverged from reality and use those insights to make subtle adjustments and course corrections to increase your strategic clarity, cut waste and seize on opportunities.

By **tracking your year-to-date income variance,** you will be able to see progress towards your goals and trends in your business. You can take into account seasonal changes to your customers' habits and get a grip on whether the business as a whole is going in the right direction.

Finally, by **tracking your balance sheet,** you'll get a powerful snapshot of your assets, liabilities and equity at a particular moment in time. This report can help you shop for a loan or prepare to sell your company.

With just those six (okay, seven!) numbers in your back pocket, you will have a huge competitive advantage over other entrepreneurs. Remember: a large business is just a small business that did the right things. If you want your business to grow and flourish, financially, you don't need an accounting degree, nor do you need to immerse yourself in a dozen finance books. These six numbers alone are all you need to get started.

The bestselling business book, *Good to Great*, examined why some companies succeed and some fail. Author Jim Collins discovered some shocking insights. He wrote:

> The good to great companies did not have a perfect track record. But on the whole, they made many more good decisions than bad ones, and they made many more good decisions than the comparison companies... This, of course, begs the question. Are we merely studying a set of companies that just happened by luck to stumble into the right decisions? Or was there something *distinctive* about their process that dramatically increased the likelihood of being right? The answer, it turns out, is that there was something quite distinctive about their process. The good to great companies display two distinctive forms of discipline thought. The first... is that they infused the entire process with the brutal facts of reality. The second... is that they developed a simple, yet deeply insightful, frame of reference for all decisions.

To bring financial clarity to your business, call Cathedral Capital, Inc. at 817.338.1011

The best way to understand the brutal facts of reality in your business is to track the numbers that we have discussed and keep a doggedly watchful eye on them as your businesses evolves. These numbers, in turn, can provide a deeply insightful frame of reference for your key financial decisions.

In other words, they can help you build what multibillionaire Warren Buffett once called the key to success at business—a durable, sustainable, long-term competitive advantage.

So what are you waiting for? Crack open QuickBooks and start crunching your numbers!

About the Author

Brooke Lively is a financial consultant specializing in closely held companies with revenues up to 10 million dollars. She advises firms to help them make the strategic financial decisions necessary to grow their businesses.

Brooke is currently serving as CFO for over thirty fast growing entrepreneurial companies around the nation. Prior to consulting, she was the full-charge administrator for a seven-figure small law firm, which she helped to create and grow from $0. She also serves as a Receiver in Texas with a special interest in family owned and operated companies and other assets in dispute. Brooke co-authored a book in 2012 on the subject of receiverships titled, *Controlling, Protecting and Monetizing Assets in Dispute.*

Before entering the legal industry she covered a wide range of public companies as an Equity Analyst with Lindus Advisors. She worked with Prides Capital and Bain Consulting where she gained corporate finance experience, working on a restructuring project involving Pegasus Solutions after it was taken private. Brooke holds an MBA with a double concentration in Investments and Corporate Finance from Texas Christian University in Fort Worth, Texas. She has been awarded the Chartered Financial Analyst designation and is a Member of the Association of Certified Fraud Examiners.

About Cathedral Capital, Inc.

We believe every company needs the guidance, support, and advice of a competent Chief Financial Officer, but few businesses can afford to employ one full time. Cathedral Capital, Inc. works with entrepreneurs who have revenues of up to ten million dollars to provide the strategic and logistical support necessary to achieve their goals – whether those are growth, succession planning, or an exit plan. We step in and assume the responsibilities of a CFO by acting as a financial steward that maintains the integrity of financial reporting and concentrates on cash, profit margins, and risk mitigation. By providing these offerings in a virtual setting, Cathedral Capital, Inc. spreads the salary expense between multiple clients and relieves the client of associated overhead. It also enables our companies to have access to individuals with specialized knowledge exactly when they need it – in a cost effective environment. Expertise when you need it without the added overhead.

To bring financial clarity to your business,
call Cathedral Capital, Inc. at 817.338.1011

DISCLAIMER for
"6 KEY NUMBERS EVERY ENTREPRENEUR SHOULD KNOW: HOW TO BRING CLARITY TO YOUR BUSINESS"

Cathedral Capital, Inc. IS PROVIDING "6 KEY NUMBERS EVERY ENTREPRENEUR SHOULD KNOW: HOW TO BRING CLARITY TO YOUR BUSINESS" (HEREAFTER REFERRED TO AS "BOOK") AND ITS CONTENTS ON AN "AS IS" BASIS AND MAKES NO REPRESENTATIONS OR WARRANTIES OF ANY KIND WITH RESPECT TO THIS BOOK OR ITS CONTENTS. CATHEDRAL CAPITAL, INC. DISCLAIMS ALL SUCH REPRESENTATIONS AND WARRANTIES, INCLUDING FOR EXAMPLE WARRANTIES OF MERCHANTABILITY AND FITNESS FOR A PARTICULAR PURPOSE. IN ADDITION, CATHEDRAL CAPITAL, INC. DOES NOT REPRESENT OR WARRANT THAT THE INFORMATION ACCESSIBLE VIA THIS BOOK IS ACCURATE, COMPLETE, OR CURRENT.

Except as specifically stated in this book, neither Cathedral Capital, Inc. nor any authors, contributors, or other representatives will be liable for damages arising out of or in connection with the use of this book. This is a comprehensive limitation of liability that applies to all damages of any kind, including (without limitation) compensatory; direct, indirect or consequential damages; loss of data, income or profit; loss of or damage to property and claims of third parties.

You understand that this book is not intended as a substitution for a consultation with an accountant.

You hereby release Cathedral Capital, Inc. and the publisher from any liability related to this book to the fullest extent permitted by law. This includes any damages, costs, or losses of any nature arising from the use of this book and the information provided by this book, including direct, consequential, special, punitive, or incidental damages, even if Cathedral Capital, Inc. has been advised of the possibility of such damages.